Ida B. Wells-Barnett

A Voice Against Violence

Patricia and Fredrick McKissack

Illustrated by Ned O.

❖ *Great African Americans Series* ❖

ENSLOW PUBLISHERS, INC.

Bloy St. & Ramsey Ave.

Box 777

Hillside, N.J. 07205

U.S.A.

Box 38

Aldershot

Hants GU12 6BP

U.K.

For Ann and Jerome Hamilton

Library of Congress Cataloging-in-Publication Data

McKissack, Pat, 1944-
    Ida B. Wells-Barnett: a voice against violence / Patricia and
Fredrick McKissack.
        p. cm. — (Great African-Americans series)
    Includes index.
    Summary: A biography of the black woman journalist who campaigned
for the civil rights of women and other minorities and was a founder
of the National Association for the Advancement of Colored People in
1909.
    ISBN 0-89490-301-2
    1. Wells-Barnett, Ida B., 1862-1931— Juvenile literature. 2. Afro-
Americans—Biography—Juvenile literature. 3. Afro-American women—
Biography—Juvenile literature. [1. Wells-Barnett, Ida B.,
1862-1931. 2. Journalists. 3. Afro-Americans—Biography.]
I. McKissack, Fredrick. II. Title. III. Series.
E185.97.W55M37   1991
323'.092—dc20
[B]   90-49848
[92]   CIP
                                                              AC

Printed in the United States of America

10 9 8 7 6 5 4 3 2 1

Photo Credits: Schomburg Center for Research in Black Culture/The New York
Public Library/Astor, Lenox and Tilden Foundations, pp. 4, 18; Department of
Special Collections, University of Chicago Library, pp. 8, 15, 20, 21, 23, 27, 29.

Illustration Credits: Ned O., pp. 6, 10, 11, 14, 16, 22, 25, 26, 28.

Cover Illustration: Ned O.

Contents

Ida B. Wells-Barnett
Born: June 1862, Holly Springs, Mississippi.
Died: March 25, 1931, Chicago, Illinois.

1

Fever!

The **Civil War*** ended in 1865, and so did **slavery** in America. Jim and Lizzie Wells were freed. So was their three-year-old daughter, Ida. The family settled in Holly Springs, Mississippi. Seven more children were born.

Ida was sent to school. Learning was

---

* Words in **bold type** are explained in *Words to Know* on page 30.

easy for her. She liked to read, but writing was more fun. She made her parents proud. Besides being smart, Ida Wells grew into a pretty girl with honey-brown skin. She was also loving and kind.

Then came the fever! **Yellow fever** was a killer **disease**. There was no cure at that time. Many good people died in Holly

Springs. Jim and Lizzie were among them. So was their baby son.

Ida was just fourteen years old. Their Holly Springs neighbors wanted to take the children to live with them. But Ida kept her family together. They lived in the house her parents left for them. She got a job as a country school teacher to earn money.

The next year, Ida let other family members take the children. Ida moved to Memphis, Tennessee and got another job teaching there.

Ida B. Wells stood up for freedom when she was very young. In 1878–79 black men and women were leaving the South. They were losing their rights. Ida wanted to stay and fight.

2

First Fight for Freedom

After the Civil War, laws were passed that protected the rights of all Americans regardless of color. Blacks had the same rights as whites. They rode in train cars together, sat together in public places, and shared the same public drinking fountains. But by 1878 laws began to change.

Ida taught in a one-room, country school just outside of Memphis. She rode the train into town at the end of each week.

One day Ida bought a train ticket to

Memphis. She took a seat in the front car. The conductor said Ida had to move to the car where men who smoked rode. It was called a **smoker car**.

Why? She was black. But it was against the law to make people sit in separate cars because of their color. Ida would not move. The conductor took her arm. She bit him. He called for help. Another man

came. They picked Ida up and made her move. No one helped her.

Ida would not sit in the smoker car. So she was put off the train.

Ida was very angry. She was just sixteen years old, but she decided to fight for her rights another way. She would take the railroad company to court. She found a lawyer to take her case. Months passed.

Nothing happened. Ida learned that her lawyer had been paid off by the railroad company. She found another lawyer.

Finally, the case went to court. Ida won her case. The judge ordered the railroad company to pay Ida $500. It was her first fight for freedom!

The railroad took the case to another court, and this time, Ida lost.

From 1880 to 1900, states passed laws that took away black people's rights. Ida would always speak out against unfair laws.

3

Violence

Ida Wells went to Rust College in Holly Springs, and Fisk University in Nashville, Tennessee.

She still taught school in Memphis. Often Ida spoke out about how poor black schools were. She wrote for a newspaper, ***The Living Word***. Ida lost her job because she spoke up about rights and fair laws.

Right away, Ida started her own newspaper, ***The Memphis Free Speech***.

In many southern states, laws were

being passed that took away the rights of African Americans. Some laws made it very hard for blacks to vote. When blacks tried to vote they were beaten. Their houses and businesses were burned. Many times they were hanged. This kind of hanging was called **lynching**.

Ida wrote about these terrible beatings,

house burnings, and lynchings. She spoke out against the unfair laws that were being passed. Friends told her to be careful. Maybe she should stop. No! She would keep writing the stories.

Then in the spring of 1892, three young

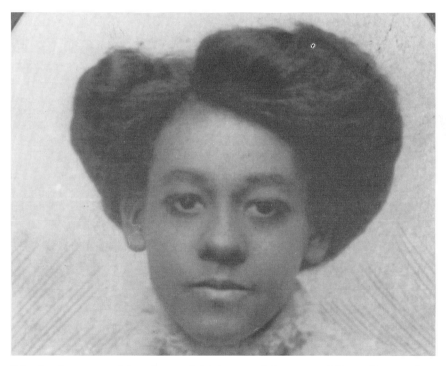

Ida had many friends and helpers. Maureen Moss Browning (above) was one of them. She helped Ida work for women's rights and against violence, too.

black men were shot to death. They had
done nothing wrong. ". . . Say or do
something," Ida wrote. Very few people
said or did anything.

Finally, a group of angry men burned

the office of *The Memphis Free Speech*. Ida got away just in time.

Running wasn't easy for Ida. She wanted to stay in Memphis, and fight against **violence**. Her friends said, go North. Go where it will be safe to speak out!

And so she did. Ida B. Wells went to New York. Her work was not over. It was really just beginning.

SOUTHERN HORRORS.

LYNCH LAW

IN ALL

ITS PHASES

Miss IDA B. WELLS,

Price, · · · Fifteen Cents.

The year Ida wrote *Southern Horrors: Lynch Law in All Its Phases* (1892) 161 blacks were lynched in the United States. She would write many books.

4

The Struggle Against Violence

Ida worked for **The New York Age** newspaper in New York. T. Thomas Fortune was the owner. He said Ida "had plenty of nerve." Those who knew Ida agreed with Mr. Fortune's words.

In 1895, Ida wrote a small book named **The Red Record**. It showed that thousands of black men, women, and children had been lynched. Something had to be done to stop the violence against black people.

Ida went all over the United States and Europe asking people to join her in her fight. Thousands and thousands of people joined her.

Ida met Ferdinand L. Barnett, a newspaper man from Chicago. They were married on June 27, 1895.

Ferdinand L. Barnett was a lawyer and a newspaper owner. After marrying Ida, Ferdinand helped with the anti-lynching work.

Many people wondered, would Ida give up her work? Not for long. When her oldest son, Charles, was six months old, Mrs. Ida Wells-Barnett went back to work. With baby Charles at her side, she spoke all over the country. She even spoke to the **president** of the United States.

Left: Ida with her oldest son, Charles, in 1896. Right: Ida with all four children in 1909, Charles, Herman, Ida, and Alfreda. Ida enjoyed her large family.

In 1898 Mrs. Wells-Barnett met with President William McKinley at the White House. She told him ten thousand black men, women, and children had been lynched since the Civil War.

The president was shocked. He made a speech against lynching. Still there was violence. The fight against it went on, too. Ida Wells-Barnett made sure of that.

Ida and Ferdinand with their children and grandchildren.

5

No More Lynching!

Ida was not the only person speaking out against lynching. Other women joined her. They formed clubs called the Ida B. Wells Clubs. *No more lynching!* was their cry.

Women could not vote. Ida worked for women's rights, too. But it wasn't until 1920 that American women were given the right to vote.

She was also interested in children's rights. Ida pushed for better laws that protected children from violence, too.

In 1909 there was a **race riot** in Springfield, Illinois. More killing . . . more burning. White and black Americans met in New York. Mrs. Ida Wells-Barnett attended. Something had to be done about the lynchings, beatings, and burnings. Out of that meeting came the **National Association for the Advancement of**

Colored People (NAACP). The NAACP was formed in 1909 to help work for rights through the courts. The NAACP also was against the **Ku Klux Klan, (KKK)** a hate group formed right after the Civil War.

For many years the KKK had not been very strong. But in 1915 the secret group started up again on Stone Mountain in Georgia. KKK members used violence

Some black soldiers were lynched after serving in World War I. Ida is shown wearing a button honoring "Negro soldiers."

and fear against people of color, Jews and Catholics.

Ida Wells-Barnett worked all her life to stop the KKK. *No more lynching!* was her battle cry.

When the spring flowers bloomed in 1931, Mrs. Wells-Barnett got sick. Two

days later, she died. Twenty years later, there was only one lynching reported in the United States. Ida's work had made a difference.

Ida B. Wells-Barnett is remembered as a woman who did much to stop violence in America. In 1990, a postage stamp was issued in her honor.

Words to Know

civil war (SIV-ill WAR)—A war fought within one country. In the United States, the Civil War was fought between Northern and Southern states.

disease—An illness or sickness.

Ku Klux Klan (KKK)—A race-hate group started after the Civil War.

The Living Word—A black-owned newspaper in Memphis, Tennessee in the 1800s.

lynching—An illegal hanging; a murder.

The Memphis Free Speech—The newspaper Ida B. Wells-Barnett began in Memphis, Tennessee.

National Association for the Advancement of Colored People (NAACP)—An organization started to help all Americans gain equal rights and protection under the law. The NAACP is one of the oldest civil rights organizations in the United States.

The New York Age—A New York newspaper owned by T. Thomas Fortune.

president (PREZ-i-dent)—The leader of a country or an organization.

race riot—Violence in the streets; violent acts against a race that has gotten out of control.

The Red Record—A book written by Ida B. Wells-Barnett in 1895.

slavery—The buying and selling of human beings.

smoker car—A train car where men who smoked had to sit. It was bad manners for men to smoke in front of women.

violence (VY-uh-lents)—Acts that hurt or destroy people, places, animals, and other things.

yellow fever—A disease that caused death at one time.

Index

**921
WEL**

McKissack, Pat.

Ida B. Wells-Barnett
: a voice against
violence.

**ANDERSON ELEMENTARY SCHOOL
HOUSTON, TEXAS 77035**

FORENSICS

by Colin Hynson

A⁺
Smart Apple Media

Published by Smart Apple Media
P.O. Box 3263, Mankato, Minnesota 56002

Series editor: Jeremy Smith
Editors: Sarah Ridley and Julia Bird
Design: sprout.uk.com
Artworks: sprout.uk.com
Picture researcher: Diana Morris

Printed in the United States of America at Corporate Graphics, in North Mankato, Minnesota.

Published by arrangement with the Watts Publishing Group LTD, London.

Library of Congress Cataloging-in-Publication Data

Hynson, Colin.
Forensics / by Colin Hynson
p. cm.—(Inside crime)
Includes index.
Summary: "Describes different forensic processes and tools used to gather and analyze evidence from crime scenes. Includes real-life case studies and examples of how crimes are solved around the world"—Provided by publisher.
ISBN 978-1-59920-394-2 (library binding)
1. Forensic sciences—Juvenile literature.
2. Evidence, Criminal—Juvenile literature. 3. Crime scene searches—Juvenile literature. 4. Forensic sciences—Case studies—Juvenile literature. I. Title.
HV8073.8.H93 2012
363.25—dc22
2010040106

1306
3-2011

9 8 7 6 5 4 3 2 1

CONTENTS

INSIDE PICTURE

Forensic scientists perform a vital role in the fight against crime. They use their scientific knowledge and expertise to investigate crimes by looking at evidence at crime scenes and taking evidence back for further work in the lab. Forensic evidence is often used in criminal trials and can help prove someone's guilt—or their innocence.

At the Scene of a Crime

For forensic scientists, it is very important that the scene of a crime is "secured" as soon as possible. This means that the crime scene is quickly closed off to everybody except those who are authorized to enter. Forensic scientists record everything at the scene that may be relevant to the crime. This might involve taking measurements, writing down notes, taking photographs, or selecting evidence to take back to the lab.

ON TARGET

In the United States, the Federal Bureau of Investigation (FBI) develops new technologies and techniques for the forensic science field in its Counterterrorism and Forensic Science Research Unit (CFSRU). The Unit's work helps both the FBI and local police departments solve crimes using the latest methods.

Back at the Lab

After the crime scene has been cleared, evidence is brought back to a lab for further investigation. Here the forensic scientists start to look for clues that will help the police link the crime to the criminal. The clues that they are looking for include traces of blood, sweat, or fingerprints. In addition, fibers from clothes or a single hair can help establish that someone was at a crime scene. Forensic scientists test any weapons found either at the scene of the crime or in the homes of suspects. If the crime is a murder, the body of the victim will undergo an autopsy. This means looking for external marks on the body or even

◀ Evidence being gathered from a crime scene by forensic scientists. They are wearing special suits, called clean suits, over their clothes to make sure that they do not contaminate the crime scene. The yellow numbered cards mark important pieces of evidence.

▶ A scene from the popular television drama about the work of forensic scientists, CSI: New York.

cutting the body open to look at the internal organs. The examination is performed by a forensic pathologist (see pages 14–15). The aim is to establish the cause and time of death.

Forensics on Television

Police dramas on television have always been very popular with viewers. In the past few years, dramas that concentrate on the work of forensic scientists have been broadcast around the world. One of the first forensic dramas was the show *Quincy M.E.* which started broadcasting in 1976. Since then, there have been the hit shows *CSI: Crime Scene Investigation, Bones,* and *NCIS.* These television shows have created a lot of interest in the work of forensic scientists. However, they have also caused something called the "CSI Effect" where the general public expects forensic science to be able to solve all crimes (which it can't) and to do so incredibly fast, as shown on television.

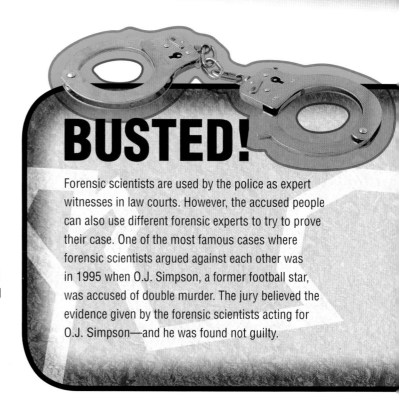

BUSTED!

Forensic scientists are used by the police as expert witnesses in law courts. However, the accused people can also use different forensic experts to try to prove their case. One of the most famous cases where forensic scientists argued against each other was in 1995 when O.J. Simpson, a former football star, was accused of double murder. The jury believed the evidence given by the forensic scientists acting for O.J. Simpson—and he was found not guilty.

FINGERPRINTING

In 1891, the Argentinian police became the first to use fingerprints to catch criminals. Now police departments worldwide keep records of fingerprints and employ scientists who are experts at finding them. Every individual has unique fingerprints, which are the patterns of ridges in the skin of the fingertips. This means that if the police have fingerprint evidence, it becomes much easier to solve a crime.

Leaving a Trace

Whenever a person's skin touches a surface, it leaves behind a faint mark. With fingerprints, this is usually a print made from the sweat or grease that lies on the surface of the skin. In addition, if people have a liquid, such as blood or ink, on their fingertips, this can leave fingerprints at the crime scene. A fingerprint that is visible to the naked eye is called a patent print, while one that appears invisible is a latent print.

When a crime scene has been secured (see pages 8, 12, and 13), the forensic scientists have to look for any fingerprints that have been left behind. If they are searching for latent fingerprints, they will use a fine brush with powder. The powder will stick to the sweat left behind. This is then lifted off using adhesive tape and taken back to the lab for analysis. Evidence taken back to the lab will also be tested for fingerprints.

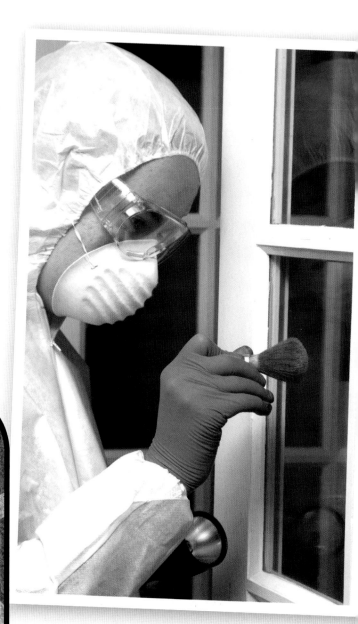

▲ Taking fingerprints is one of the most important parts of investigating a crime scene. This forensic scientist is brushing powder over the glass of a window, checking for fingerprints.

FACT FILE

Fingerprints are usually a reliable way of catching criminals. However, occasionally mistakes are made. In 1997, Stephan Cowan was arrested for a shooting in Boston, Massachusetts, after a fingerprint was found at the scene of the crime that appeared to match his. Cowan protested his innocence but was sent to prison. Eventually, the police agreed to analyze his fingerprints again. The investigation showed that the fingerprint actually belonged to a hostage, and Cowan was not at the crime scene. After serving six years in prison, Cowan was released.

Matching the Prints

Once fingerprints have been found, they have to be compared with all the fingerprints that the police have on record. This is done by looking for similarities between the two prints. The more similarities that exist, the more likely it becomes that the prints are the same. Today there are computer programs that can compare fingerprints, speeding up the process.

Looking in the Database

Fingerprints are only useful as evidence if the police are able to match any fingerprints found at a crime scene to fingerprints that they have in their records. Most countries now have the fingerprint records of everybody who has been convicted of a crime. Some countries retain the fingerprint records of anybody who has been arrested for a recordable crime. This causes unease for some who see it as an attack on personal privacy and freedom. Others think that everybody's fingerprint records should be taken so that there are no gaps in the records.

ON TARGET

In the United States, the Federal Bureau of Investigation (FBI) maintains the Integrated Automated Fingerprint Identification System. This is a computer database with the fingerprints of over 55 million Americans. It is available to police forces across the U.S. and can usually make a match within two hours.

▼ When somebody is fingerprinted in a police station, it is important that all 10 fingerprints are taken. This is because each finger has a slightly different fingerprint pattern.

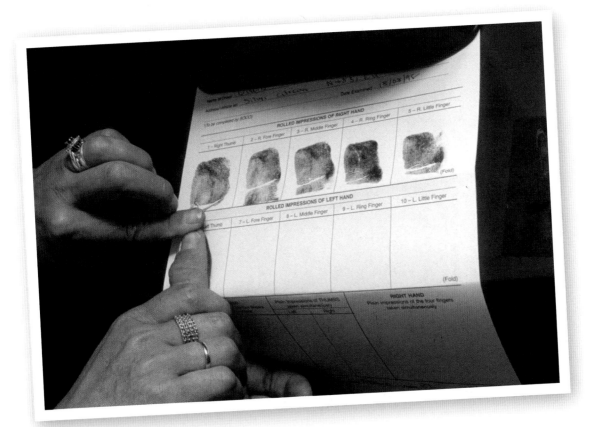

SECURING THE CRIME SCENE

When forensic science was in its infancy, it was usually police officers who looked for evidence at the scene of a crime. There was no attempt to make the area secure. Police officers would walk around the crime scene and handle evidence without any supervision. As forensic science developed, it became more important that the whole area was closely controlled.

The "Golden Hour"

When the police arrive at the scene of a major crime, such as a murder, they make sure that there is no one in danger and that anyone injured is being treated. At that point, they rope off the area and only allow in authorized personnel, such as forensic scientists. Speed is now important. Police officers need to question any witnesses while their memories are still clear. Evidence must be preserved by forensic scientists before it is altered by weather or time. This is known as the "Golden Hour."

▼ Although speed is important for forensic scientists, the crime scene is preserved for as long as possible so that more detailed investigations can take place. An outline of the victim's body has been marked so that the forensic scientists can remember how the body fell.

ON TARGET

In August 2005, Hurricane Katrina passed through the city of New Orleans causing terrible floods. In the days that followed, over 700 people died. After the flood waters retreated, forensic investigators were brought in to confirm that the dead had been killed by the storm. As a result of their investigations, they began several murder investigations, since some of the deaths looked suspicious.

▲ Securing an outside crime scene needs to be done at a fast pace because changing weather and pollution may contaminate the evidence very quickly. Each yellow letter is linked to a piece of evidence that has been taken away.

Recording the Scene

Once the forensic scientists arrive at a crime scene, they start to record all of the evidence that they can find. They take photographs of the scene from every angle, draw a map of the area marking anything that they think is relevant to the police investigation, and collect evidence to take back to the lab. Sometimes police officers make a thorough search for clues. They have to crawl along on their hands and knees looking for potential evidence. In some crimes, the police do not know what they are looking for, but anything found is recorded in case it turns out to be important in later investigations.

Dressing for the Scene

Whenever people walk into a crime scene, they will leave something behind, such as fibers from their clothes, mud from their shoes, or even some hair. Any of these might contaminate the crime scene and slow down the investigation. Everybody who enters the crime scene should wear a clean suit that covers them from head to toe. They should also wear special shoes or overshoes to prevent contamination and to help identify their footprints.

BUSTED!

In November 2008, British man Peter Mahoney was arrested for an armed carjacking. When the burned-out car was found, forensic scientists discovered some hairs that had survived the flames. These hairs came from a dog. When Mahoney was arrested, a vet took a hair sample from his dog, Buster. The hair matched those found in the car. This forensic evidence was used to link Mahoney to the crime. He was found guilty and sent to jail for four years.

THE AUTOPSY

A postmortem (after death) examination, or autopsy, takes place in order to find out why somebody died, especially if their death was sudden or suspicious. Autopsies are also used to identify a body if it has been badly burned in a fire or if the body has decomposed. These examinations are carried out by specialists called forensic pathologists.

External Examination

When a body is brought into an autopsy room, an assessment of the body is made. The forensic pathologist will look for clues such as cuts, bruises, or other marks on the skin. Every mark will be recorded with photos and written notes. If there are stab wounds or bullet holes on the body, they are studied as well. These wounds can show what angle the dead person was attacked at and how deep the wound went. In many cases, an external examination is only the start of the investigation, as more clues about somebody's death can be found inside the body.

FACT FILE

One of the main purposes of an autopsy is to determine the cause of death. This is especially important if the death appears suspicious. The pathologist will make a detailed examination of the outside and the inside of the body. The autopsy should reveal whether the victim died of natural causes (old age or undiagnosed illness), was murdered, committed suicide, or died accidentally. On some rare occasions, no cause of death can be found.

▼ *Pathologists carry out an autopsy. An autopsy is performed to establish the cause of death or to increase the knowledge of a fatal disease.*

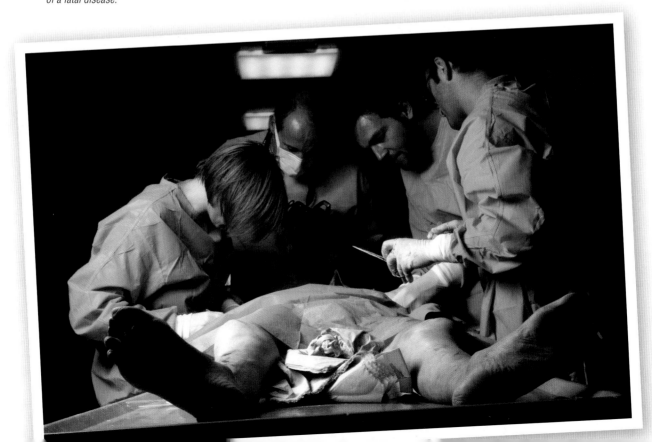

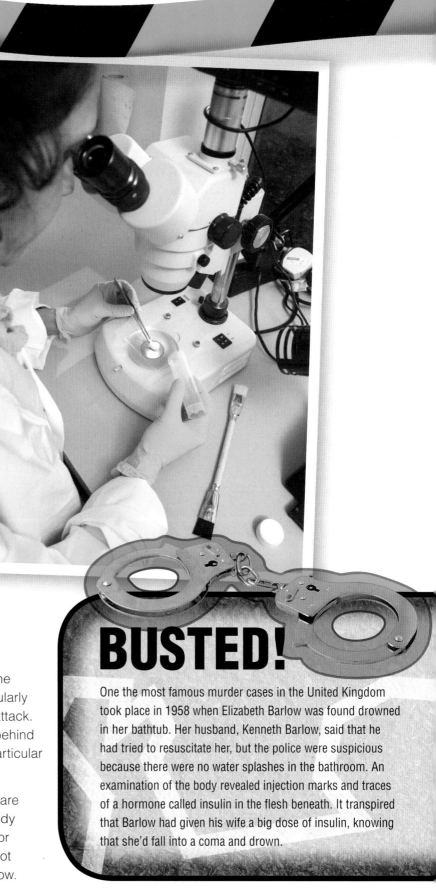

▶ Examining bones under a microscope can give many clues as to the cause of death. A stabbing or a shooting can damage bones, and it may be possible to match this damage to a weapon.

Opening Up the Body

When all the information from an external examination has been recorded, the pathologist may start an examination of the internal organs of the body. Pathologists use special saws to cut through the rib cage. After this, the organs, such as the heart, lungs, and stomach, can be removed for closer examination. Half-digested food inside the stomach will tell the pathologist the last thing that somebody ate before death and how long it had been in the stomach. This can help to establish a time of death.

One major cause of violent death is bleeding inside the skull after a heavy blow to the head. To find out if this did cause death, the brain has to be removed and examined.

Along with the internal organs, the bones of the dead can also reveal evidence. This is particularly useful when looking at victims of a stabbing attack. Stab wounds can damage bones and leave behind a mark. These marks can sometimes link a particular weapon to the stabbing.

Once the autopsy is over, the internal organs are carefully replaced inside the body and the body is sewn up. The body is stored in a mortuary or morgue at a low temperature so that it does not decompose. Burial or cremation can then follow.

BUSTED!

One the most famous murder cases in the United Kingdom took place in 1958 when Elizabeth Barlow was found drowned in her bathtub. Her husband, Kenneth Barlow, said that he had tried to resuscitate her, but the police were suspicious because there were no water splashes in the bathroom. An examination of the body revealed injection marks and traces of a hormone called insulin in the flesh beneath. It transpired that Barlow had given his wife a big dose of insulin, knowing that she'd fall into a coma and drown.

NATURAL CLUES: INSECTS

When somebody dies, his or her body starts to release foul-smelling chemicals, such as cadaverine and putrescine. These chemicals attract insects to the corpse. Some of these insects will eat the decaying flesh that they find. Other insects will lay eggs on the corpse so that their newly hatched young will have a ready supply of food. Experts called forensic entomologists study these insects and use them to figure out when somebody died.

The Arrival of the Insects

The first insects to arrive at a dead body are usually flies. There are many different types of flies, including blowflies or house flies, which will use a dead body as a host for their eggs. The emerging maggots can then feed on the body. About a week later, beetles and mites follow. These insects will either lay their eggs on the body, eat the decomposing flesh, or eat the maggots that are on the body. As the body reaches the final stages of decomposition, clothes moths are attracted to the body to feed on the corpse's hair or fur. The presence (or absence) of these different insects can help to establish the time of death.

▶ *Whenever anything living dies, it immediately becomes a source of food for insects or their young. Maggots swarm over this decaying sheep's head.*

BUSTED!

Evidence from forensic entomology was used during the trial of David Westerfield of San Diego, California, in 2002. He was accused of murdering 7-year-old Danielle Van Dam. Both the prosecution and the defense used forensic entomologists to determine when Danielle Van Dam died. They disagreed about the age of fly larvae found on the body. The prosecution won the case and Westerfield was found guilty.

▼ One of the ways in which forensic entomologists can determine the time of a death is to identify the flies that have settled on the body and what stage of their life cycle has been reached. Some flies are taken back to the lab for further examination under a microscope.

Life Cycles

Forensic entomologists study the life cycles of insects. An adult fly will lay her eggs around any openings in the dead body, such as the ears or nose. In 24 hours, these will hatch into maggots (larvae). As the maggots feed on the corpse, they grow and molt their skin twice. After about 10 days, the maggots turn into pupae. This stage lasts about a week and then the adult flies emerge. These flies are ready to lay their own eggs in just one day. So if a forensic entomologist finds the pupae, for instance, of a particular fly on a dead body, it helps to establish a possible time of death.

Other Crimes

As well as murder investigations, forensic entomologists are used in several different types of criminal cases. They can be used when the police are investigating the neglect of animals or the neglect of vulnerable people, such as children or the elderly. They can also be used to investigate illegal goods. Any insects on these goods could tell the police where the goods first came from.

ON TARGET

In 1995, police in Canada became concerned that bears were being shot so that their gall bladders could be removed. They believed that the gall bladders were being smuggled to Asia to be used in traditional medicine. In July 1995, two dead bears were found. The insects on the bodies were investigated to establish a time of death. This evidence helped link the bears' deaths to two men who were in the area at the time when the bears were known to have died.

SOILS AND SEEDS

Natural materials, such as soil, seeds, or pollen, can be very useful to forensic scientists. Many of these materials stick to people very easily, especially on their shoes and clothes, and will also fall off. By analyzing natural materials gathered from a crime scene, forensic scientists can sometimes find out where a murder took place and if a suspect was at the scene of the crime.

Different Kinds of Soil

Police can use experts called forensic geologists to study soil samples and other natural materials taken from a crime scene. There are many different kinds of soil, even within quite a small area, and other natural materials such as leaves or seeds can only be found in certain places and at certain times of the year. For instance, if a particular pollen spore is found at a crime scene, forensic scientists can use it to identify a plant. Since each plant produces pollen at particular times of the year, pollen samples can give important clues about when the crime occurred and even the whereabouts of either the suspect or the victim.

BUSTED!

In September 2000, a woman and her son went missing in south Australia. Their car was found with a muddy shovel inside it, but with no sign of the two missing people. An analysis of the soil that was stuck to the blade of the shovel led the police to a quarry, where they found the buried bodies of the missing people. This evidence also led to the arrest of a man for the double murder.

▼ Grains of pollen under a microscope. If pollen is found at a crime scene, then simply identifying which plant the pollen came from helps to establish when a crime was committed.

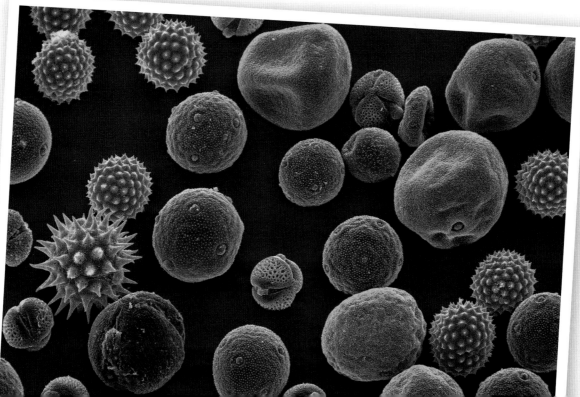

▼ Boots and shoes can provide all sorts of clues for forensic scientists. Some of the more useful clues can be found on the soles. Soil and seeds can often be found stuck to shoes and may link a suspect to the scene of the crime, leading to an arrest.

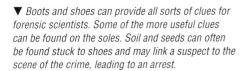

ON TARGET

The FBI has its own forensic science lab in Quantico, Virginia. One group of FBI scientists works at the Trace Evidence Unit. It analyzes and compares any small materials found during a crime investigation. The Trace Evidence Unit works on about 2,000 cases every year.

Looking for Materials

Forensic scientists looking for soil and seed clues will look in a variety of places, not just at the scene of a crime. If the crime is a murder, it may be that the victim was killed in one location and moved to another. Analyzing samples from victims, clothes, hair, and fingernails might reveal where they died. A suspect's clothes, home, and even car may also be inspected in order to establish if he or she was at the scene of a crime at a particular time.

One of the first times that seeds helped convict a murder suspect was in 1942. Some grass seeds were found on the clothes of a murder suspect. A botanist looked at the seeds and discovered that the kind of grass the seeds came from was very rare and could only be found in a few places. One of those places was the scene of the murder. On top of that, the seeds were only produced in one month every year. It was the same month that the murder was committed.

USING BLOOD

Whenever a violent attack is being investigated by the police, it is likely that there will be blood at the scene of the crime. This may be the blood of the victim or, if there was a struggle, of the attacker. Any blood found as part of a crime scene investigation will be examined, as it can reveal all sorts of clues.

Testing the Blood

If an attack took place some time before the police arrived, any blood at the scene would have dried out and would simply appear as a stain. Therefore, the first thing that needs to be done is for an expert called a forensic serologist to test the stain for blood using the Kastle-Meyer Test. If the stain turns out to be blood, a sample is taken to the lab for further analysis.

▼ *Karl Landsteiner's discovery of blood types not only helped forensic scientists with their work but also made blood transfusions possible. The first blood transfusion took place in 1907.*

In 1902, an Austrian scientist named Karl Landsteiner (see photo) discovered that human blood could be broken up into four main types: A, B, AB, and O. This is known as the ABO grouping. Everybody's blood belongs to one of these types. A lab can use a process called electrophoresis to establish to which type a blood sample belongs. However, because so many people share the same blood type, it cannot be used by itself to prove someone's identity. It can help to narrow down the suspects, in the case of the attacker, or to help to identify the victim.

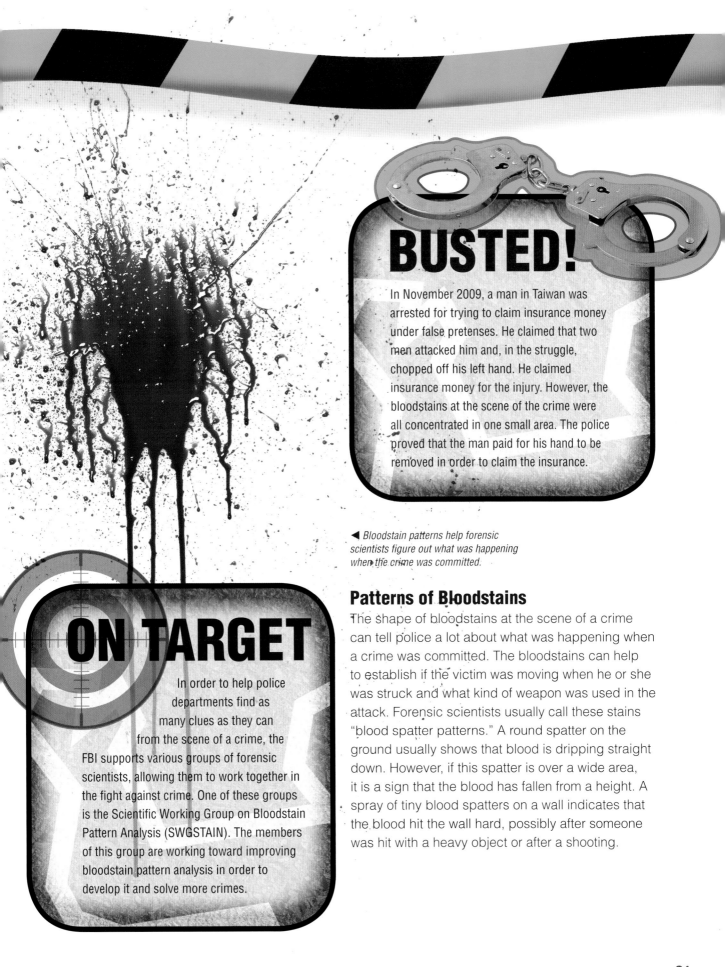

Bloodstain patterns help forensic scientists figure out what was happening when the crime was committed.

BUSTED!

In November 2009, a man in Taiwan was arrested for trying to claim insurance money under false pretenses. He claimed that two men attacked him and, in the struggle, chopped off his left hand. He claimed insurance money for the injury. However, the bloodstains at the scene of the crime were all concentrated in one small area. The police proved that the man paid for his hand to be removed in order to claim the insurance.

ON TARGET

In order to help police departments find as many clues as they can from the scene of a crime, the FBI supports various groups of forensic scientists, allowing them to work together in the fight against crime. One of these groups is the Scientific Working Group on Bloodstain Pattern Analysis (SWGSTAIN). The members of this group are working toward improving bloodstain pattern analysis in order to develop it and solve more crimes.

Patterns of Bloodstains

The shape of bloodstains at the scene of a crime can tell police a lot about what was happening when a crime was committed. The bloodstains can help to establish if the victim was moving when he or she was struck and what kind of weapon was used in the attack. Forensic scientists usually call these stains "blood spatter patterns." A round spatter on the ground usually shows that blood is dripping straight down. However, if this spatter is over a wide area, it is a sign that the blood has fallen from a height. A spray of tiny blood spatters on a wall indicates that the blood hit the wall hard, possibly after someone was hit with a heavy object or after a shooting.

DNA EVIDENCE

The use of DNA (deoxyribonucleic acid) fingerprinting has revolutionized the way in which police departments can solve crimes. DNA is made up of a long string of molecules inside every single cell in the human body. It carries information about how our bodies are built, such as height, hair color, and resistance to various diseases. Only identical twins or triplets carry the same DNA. Everybody else carries his or her own unique set of DNA molecules inside every cell. Scientists can use "DNA fingerprints" to identify someone, just like they can with actual fingerprints.

The Invention of DNA Fingerprinting

In 1985, Professor Sir Alec Jeffreys discovered a way to extract DNA from cells and compare it with another DNA set. Using this technique, it is possible to see whether DNA found at a crime scene matches that of anybody linked to a crime scene.

ON TARGET

Police departments around the world are building up databases of DNA fingerprints. This means that if a DNA sample is found at a crime scene, they can simply make a comparison with all the DNA on file. The largest DNA database in the world is CODIS and is run by the FBI. As of 2010, the database contained over 8.6 million offender profiles and produced over 120,000 hits. At that time, over 170 public law enforcement labs across the country used the database.

It was first used to solve two murders: one committed in 1983 and another in 1986. A man had confessed to both killings, but Jeffreys compared the man's DNA with some found at both murder scenes and proved that he did not commit the crimes. The same DNA sample eventually led to the arrest of another man.

◄ *Any DNA fingerprints that are created from DNA samples have to be compared with a huge database of DNA fingerprints. The best way to do this is to turn the DNA fingerprint into a visual form so that a comparison can be made. Alec Jeffreys is shown here comparing two DNA fingerprints.*

Extracting DNA

Two years before Alec Jeffreys developed DNA fingerprinting, scientist Kary Mullis invented the Polymerase Chain Reaction (PCR). This allowed scientists to isolate the specific piece of DNA that they were interested in and make as many copies of it as they needed. First, a forensic scientist takes a cell sample and purifies it to get rid of any impurities. It is then mixed with chemicals that extract the DNA. The sample is put into a PCR machine which "amplifies" the DNA. This means that it makes copies of the DNA many thousands of times until there is enough DNA material for scientists to work with.

Short Tandem Repeat Profiling

Once the DNA has been copied in the PCR machine, it has to be put into a visual form so that a comparison can be made. The most common technique for this is known as Short Tandem Repeat (STR) profiling. As with DNA fingerprinting, it allows a scientist to compare repeated short sections of DNA extracted from a DNA sample by turning it

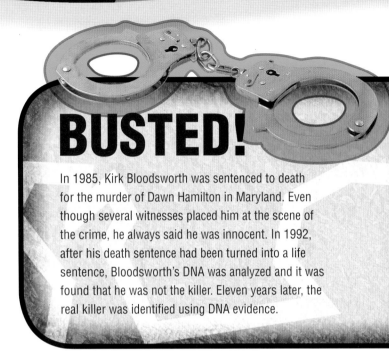

BUSTED!

In 1985, Kirk Bloodsworth was sentenced to death for the murder of Dawn Hamilton in Maryland. Even though several witnesses placed him at the scene of the crime, he always said he was innocent. In 1992, after his death sentence had been turned into a life sentence, Bloodsworth's DNA was analyzed and it was found that he was not the killer. Eleven years later, the real killer was identified using DNA evidence.

into long bar codes or graphs. Then the scientist can compare the different DNA samples to see which ones match.

▼ The amount of DNA found at a crime scene is usually very small so it is important that the DNA is replicated. This is done using a PCR machine. Each of the small tubes below will create a new DNA set.

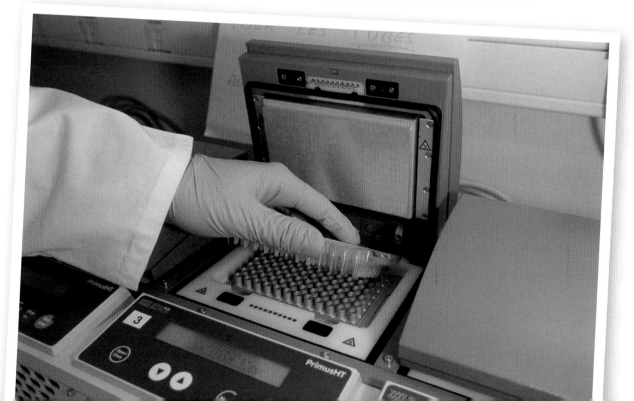

BONES AND SKULLS

One group of forensic scientists, known as forensic anthropologists, study human remains a long time after death has taken place. In the case of dead bodies, the bones and skull last long after the rest of the body has decomposed. Studying these bones can help to establish the age, sex, ethnic origin, and cause of death of the dead person.

Studying the Bones

If a dead body has been reduced to a skeleton, these remains are laid out for examination on a mortuary table. Because skeletons change throughout a person's life, it is possible to figure out the age of the person who died. Pelvic bones in men and women are a different size and shape, so the gender of the skeleton can also be identified. The skull helps with finding out about the ethnic origin of the skeleton. The skulls of Europeans tend to be different from those of either Africans or Asians. However, skull shape is not always a reliable indicator of ethnic origin, as there are wide variations within each ethnic group. If the bones show any signs of disease, that can also help to identify individuals.

BUSTED!

In 1994, an Argentinian forensic anthropology team examined the 200 victims of a massacre that took place in the Guatemalan village of Dos Erres in 1982. Their findings led to the arrest of a Guatemalan soldier who was living in the United States in May 2010. He was charged with their murders.

▶ Forensic anthropologists at work in Bosnia-Herzegovina in 2005. They make detailed records before moving a skeleton from its burial site. In this case, their investigations helped to solve a war crime.

War Crimes

One area of work for forensic anthropologists is in the field of solving war crimes. Since the 1990s there have been conflicts around the world where civilians have been rounded up, executed, and buried in mass graves. Forensic anthropologists have worked in countries such as Rwanda, Kosovo, Bosnia-Herzegovina, and various countries in South America (see box to the right). They examine the scattered bones found in these mass graves. Using these bones, they can figure out the time and cause of death. They also try to reunite as many bones as possible so that the bodies can be buried properly.

Waking the Dead

Sometimes the only way to identify a dead person is to use the skull to reconstruct the face. Traditionally, this is done by adding layers of clay to the skull. The amount of flesh and muscle to be added is done by using the same amount as would normally be seen on a person of the same age and sex. The person making the facial reconstruction has to make an educated guess about hair or skin color. Today, facial reconstructions are made using data from CT (computerized tomography) scans of people with a similar skull size and shape. Facial details such as skin, eye color, and hair are added.

ON TARGET

The Argentine Forensic Anthropology Team works internationally on war crime and human rights cases. They have helped to identify individuals in Bolivia, El Salvador, Colombia, East Timor, Chile, and Lebanon. In each of these cases, they were able to identify many of the victims of these crimes, so family members could take them away for a proper burial.

▼ A forensic scientist reconstructs the features of a face. The scientist has already scanned the skull shape into the computer and built up layers of muscle digitally.

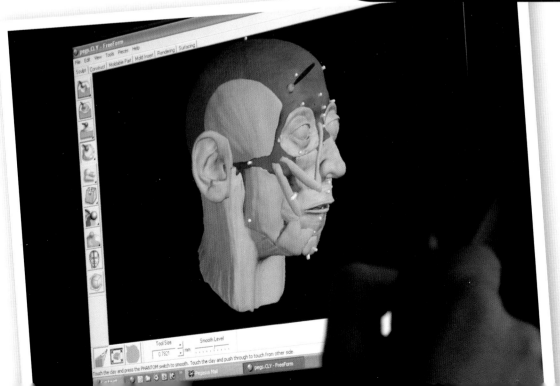

CASE STUDY:
THE BODY FARM

The "Body Farm" is officially called the Forensic Anthropology Center at the University of Tennessee. It has proven to be an invaluable source of information for forensic scientists, particularly forensic anthropologists, around the world. The Body Farm studies the way that human bodies decompose in different environments. The results of these studies allow forensic anthropologists to make a more accurate assessment of the time of death.

The Beginnings

The Forensic Anthropology Center was started in 1971 by William M. Bass. Bass had just started as Professor of Anthropology at the University of Tennessee and had become the first forensic anthropologist for the state of Tennessee. It was his forensic anthropology work that convinced him that more research was needed into how bodies decompose when they are placed in different environments—and so the Body Farm was born.

▼ Corpses in the Body Farm are wrapped up in different materials, such as cloth or plastic. Each body is then checked to see how the materials have affected the way that the body has decomposed.

Inside the Body Farm

The Body Farm occupies an area of about 108,000 square feet (10,000 sq. m). The whole area is surrounded by a high wall which is topped with razor wire. This is designed to keep out anybody who might break in and contaminate the bodies inside. In 2008, there were about 650 skeletons inside the Center. Some of these are unidentified bodies from local morgues, but most of the bodies come from people who had agreed to donate their bodies to the Center after death. About 100 people each year agree that the Center can use their bodies after death.

The Work of the Body Farm

The bodies inside the Center are studied as they decompose. Bodies are covered in plastic sheets or are left exposed. They are placed in the full sun or in the shade. Some of the bodies are buried, placed in a tub full of water, or put into the trunk of a car. Scientists at the Center watch carefully as the bodies begin to decay. They note physical changes to the bodies, the amount of insect activity, and the speed of decomposition. All of this information is entered into a computer database. They have also begun to research the smells released during decomposition so that dogs can be trained to search for corpses.

ON TARGET

The Center has been so successful that there are plans to expand it to nearly 538,000 square feet (50,000 sq. m). At the same time, new Body Farms have started at three more universities. The different temperatures and local environments at these universities will mean that the results of their studies will differ from those in Tennessee.

◀ The current head of the Forensic Anthropology Center, Dr. Richard Jantz. He helps many police departments with their crime scene investigations.

BUSTED!

In December 1993, "Big Mike" Rubenstein called the police to tell them that he had found the bodies of three of his relatives in a cabin. He said that he had visited the cabin in November but that it was empty. The police investigated the deaths and became suspicious, especially after Rubenstein quickly applied for life insurance payments on his dead relatives. They called in staff from the Body Farm. Their knowledge of body decomposition showed that the people had been killed in November 1993. "Big Mike" Rubenstein was convicted of their murders.

CLOTHES AND SHOES

It was the French forensic scientist Edmond Locard who created the principle that every forensic scientist knows—"every contact leaves a trace." In other words, whenever two people or materials touch, material is transferred from one to the other. This can include natural materials left behind on shoes or clothes, or the fibers that fall off a person's clothing.

▲ Examining prints left behind by boots and shoes can help to find out if a suspect was at the scene of a crime. Different shoes have different designs on their soles.

Leaving a Print

One of the things that forensic scientists look for when a crime scene is secured is shoe or boot prints. However, prints like these are not likely to remain fresh for long, so it is vital that they are recorded quickly. First a cast of the print is made using a liquid plastic resin. When this hardens, it is taken to the lab, where another cast is made from the resin cast. This time a hard material such as plaster of paris is used.

Once the cast of the shoe print is ready, it can be examined for clues. One of the things that forensic scientists look out for is any signs of wear and tear.

ON TARGET

The FBI maintains a database of the prints made by shoe and boot soles and heels. This allows police departments to make a comparison between prints found at crime scenes and in the database. Fashions in shoes, especially tennis shoes, change fast, so it is important that shoe manufacturers let the FBI know about any new designs as they appear.

These will usually be unique to a particular shoe, so it is fairly easy to match it to the suspect's shoes. If the scientists wants to know the make of shoe, they can look at the patterns on the sole and match it to one kind of shoe.

Comparing Fibers

One type of clue that suspected criminals leave behind are fibers from their clothes. Clothes are made from different materials, such as cotton or wool, and have been dyed various colors. If any fibers are found at the scene of the crime, they can be compared with fibers from the clothes of any suspects. This can be done with a comparison microscope, a kind of double microscope that allows two fiber samples to be viewed at the same time. If a match is made, this can help to place a suspect at a crime scene. If a forensic scientist has only one fiber to work with, he or she can use a FTIR (Fourier Transform Infrared spectroscopy) machine. This machine examines the fiber using different wavelengths of light. The result can then be compared to a database of materials.

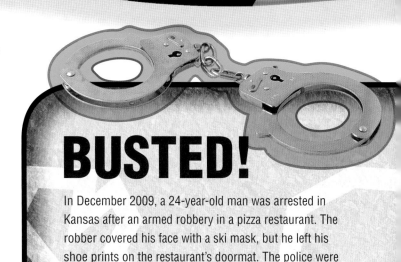

BUSTED!

In December 2009, a 24-year-old man was arrested in Kansas after an armed robbery in a pizza restaurant. The robber covered his face with a ski mask, but he left his shoe prints on the restaurant's doormat. The police were able to match these prints with the shoe prints of one of their suspects.

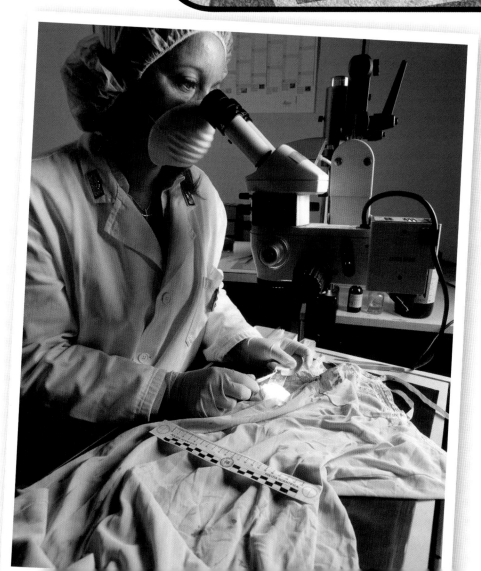

▶ *A forensic scientist collects evidence from a bloodstained dress. She is using a microscope to collect single hairs or fibers from the dress.*

PAPER TRAIL

Some crimes are almost impossible to spot. There are criminals who are experts at forgery, producing fake money, documents, or works of art. Forensic scientists work to uncover these forgeries. They also examine any pieces of paper at a crime scene, searching for hidden clues such as the impression of writing that cannot be seen by the naked eye.

▲ *These euros (left) contain watermarks, microletters, and thin metal strips that make them very difficult, or too expensive, for forgers to copy. Even still, the counterfeit bills on the right look very much like the real thing.*

Revealing the Forgery

Dollar bills are printed in special, highly secure buildings called mints. The bills that they produce are printed so that they are almost impossible to forge. However, this does not stop some criminals from printing their own money and trying to get it past people who are too busy or careless to check it properly. If a forensic scientist is given a bill to examine, there are various things that he or she can look for.

Real bills use a type of paper that is difficult for the public to obtain. During the printing process, microletters are added that can only be seen with a magnifying glass. There are also some features of the bill that can only be seen under an ultraviolet light.

BUSTED!

The Chinese police broke up a money forgery ring in April 2009. At the start of the year, fake bills were circulating around various regions in China. The fake bills had a face value of $26 million. After using forensic techniques that found the forgeries used the wrong kind of paper, the Chinese police were able to seize the counterfeit cash and arrest over 600 people.

The Age of Paper, Paint, and Ink

Forgeries of paintings, books, or documents are sometimes difficult to detect. The materials used to create the forgery can be examined to determine when they were made. For instance, in 1981 the diaries of Adolf Hitler were "discovered" by a journalist in Germany. Handwriting experts and a well-known historian said that the diaries were real. However, an examination by forensic experts found that the paper and ink used in the diaries were modern and were not available in Hitler's time. The journalist, Gerd Heidemann, and the forger, Konrad Kujau (see photo), were each given prison sentences for their part in the hoax.

The Electrostatic Detective

Whenever somebody writes on a notepad, a very faint copy of what was written is left on the sheet under the paper that was first used. If forensic investigators are searching for hidden writing, they can use a machine called an ESDA (Electrostatic Detection Apparatus). A thin piece of film is laid over the paper, and an electric charge is then passed through the film. The electrical charge is strongest on top of where the hidden writing is on the paper. Powder is then scattered over the film, and the excess is blown away. The powder that is left behind will reveal the writing on the paper.

FACT FILE

In November 2006, the Victoria and Albert Museum in London held an exhibition of forged paintings that looked like works of art by such great painters as Picasso, Matisse, and Ben Nicholson. The exhibition was organized by London's Metropolitan Police Force's Arts and Antiques Unit. Its aim was to show the public just how difficult it is to spot an art forgery.

◀ The Hitler diaries were created by a forger named Konrad Kujau. He is shown holding letters that he said proved that the diaries were real. The letters and the diary were fake, and Kujau was sent to prison for 48 months.

GUNS AND BULLETS

If a gun is used during a crime, then a lot of clues will be left behind, even if the gun has been taken away from the crime scene. As soon as the crime scene is secured, the forensic team starts to search for evidence of the shooting that took place. These investigations continue in the lab.

Evidence at the Crime Scene

After a shooting incident, forensic scientists will look for evidence to help establish the exact location of the victim and the suspected shooter. They will examine the position of the body of the victim, any blood spattered around the crime scene, bullet holes, used bullets, and bullet cases.

Blood spatters on a wall can show forensic experts from which direction the gun was fired. Any bullet cases will show the police where the gun was fired from. The position and angle of any bullet holes can also show where the gunshot came from.

ON TARGET

The FBI's Firearms-Toolmarks Unit (FTU) examines firearms, toolmarks, and ammunition found at a crime scene. The agents in this unit examine bullets found in bodies to try to match them to a gun. They also look at gunshot patterns and the residue left behind by gun powder to determine how a crime was committed.

▼ A bullet hole in a tree trunk has been marked up by a forensic scientist. There is a vertical and a horizontal ruler so that the hole can be measured. The hole has been taped up to protect it from the weather.

▲ *A forensic scientist examines the bottom of a bullet case, using his computer to view the magnified image.*

Evidence in the Lab

It is unusual for the gun used in a crime to have been left at the crime scene. However, the bullets and bullet cases found at the crime scene can be examined because different types of guns use different types of bullets. Identifying the bullet that was used by the criminal will narrow down the types of guns that could have been used to fire the bullet.

When a bullet is fired out of a gun, grooves inside the barrel of the gun leave marks on the bullet. These marks are called striations. The firing pin inside the gun also leaves a small hole in the bullet case. Like fingerprints or DNA, the marks and holes are unique to each gun, and the same striations are left every time the gun is fired.

The Shooting Bath

If the suspect of a shooting is found with a gun, it is imperative to find out if this was the same gun that was used in the crime. The gun is brought to the forensic lab where it is fired into a large tank filled with water for safety and in order to collect

the fired bullet. Using a comparison microscope, the scientists can then compare the bullets and cases fired in the lab with any bullets and cases found at the crime scene. If the striations and holes are the same, they know that they have the gun used at the crime.

BUSTED!

In April 2010, 39-year-old Stephan J. Tamburo III of West Virginia was arrested for the murder of his father. The murder took place in December 2008, but the body was not found until April 2009. DNA samples from the body proved the identity of the victim, and bullets in the body were matched to a gun in his son's home.

DRUGS AND POISONS

If drug use or poisons are suspected in a crime, scientists called toxicologists are called in to help identify the toxins used. A toxin is any substance harmful to the human body. Toxicologists analyze unknown powders or liquids to identify drugs, as well as substances or poisons used to kill someone.

Drugs and Crime

Most drug crime is linked to the production, trafficking, and selling of illegal drugs. In order to bring drug criminals to court, law enforcement agencies often use the skills of toxicologists to analyze substances found on the suspect or at the crime scene in order to prove guilt. In addition, driving under the influence of drugs or alcohol is against the law. Levels of alcohol or drugs in the body can be tested using roadside tests. Police may take saliva, urine, or blood samples from a suspect for further analysis by a toxicologist.

◄ *Bottles of arsenic and capsicum from the 1920s. The bottle on the left, containing arsenic, is a special shape and color, with the word "poison" embossed in the glass, for ease of identification. The one on the right does not contain poison.*

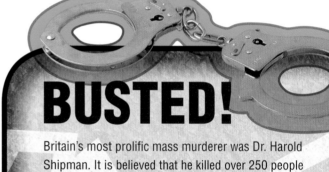

BUSTED!

Britain's most prolific mass murderer was Dr. Harold Shipman. It is believed that he killed over 250 people that were in his care. The police became involved after it was noticed that a large number of his patients were dying. An examination of his last victim found a large amount of a drug called diamorphine in her body. Shipman was eventually convicted of the murder of 15 more of his patients, who all died after a drug overdose administered by Dr. Shipman.

Killing with Poison

In the past, poison was one of the most favored ways of killing a victim. Poisons, such as arsenic, strychnine, and antimony, were used to commit murder. With today's sophisticated forensic science, it would be very difficult for anybody to get away with murder by poisoning. However, in 1978, Georgi Markov, a Bulgarian communist defector living in London, was killed by poisoning. On his way to work in 1978, he felt a jab in the leg. He turned to see somebody pick up an umbrella and walk away. Three days later, Markov was dead. A tiny pellet containing the poison ricin was found in his body. The pellet had been stabbed into him with the umbrella. His killer was never caught, as the Bulgarian authorities denied any knowledge of the murder and refused to cooperate.

Testing for Toxins

An important part of a forensic toxicologist's job is to identify any drugs or poisons linked to a crime by testing unknown substances found at the crime scene, or detecting drugs or poisons in body fluids, tissues, or organs. One of the best ways of doing this is to use a mass spectrometer which rapidly screens for a range of drugs and poisons, even if they are present in tiny quantities. It does this by breaking a substance up into its separate molecules. Once the molecules are separated, they can be examined and any toxins can be identified.

ON TARGET

Police departments around the world have special forensic teams that are experts in toxicology. The FBI has a Chemistry Unit which works in the field of toxicology. They have special equipment that is not normally available to police departments, and they assist at crime scenes where the use of poisons is suspected.

▼ *A chemist places samples in a mass spectrometer in order to identify all the substances contained in each sample.*

CRASH INVESTIGATIONS

Any major vehicle crash is investigated to see if the cause of the crash can be established. Forensic scientists have to discover if the crash was accidental, deliberate, or caused by carelessness. They do this by gradually piecing together the chain of events that led to the crash.

Car Crashes

If there is a car crash or an incident that involves several vehicles, one of the things that the forensic scientists will look for are the skid marks on the road. The skid marks are caused when drivers suddenly brake but the vehicles keep moving. The length of a skid mark can show how fast the vehicle was traveling at the time of the crash. A curvy skid mark suggests that the driver was not in control of his or her vehicle. If the skid marks start too close to an obstruction, they may indicate that the driver was not paying attention while driving. Forensic investigators can also recreate crashes using crash test dummies.

ON TARGET

There are several private companies that specialize in investigating car crashes. Businesses such as Crash Forensics in Kansas work with both the police and insurance companies to find out how a crash actually took place. Along with skid marks, they also analyze the vehicles in the crash and even create a computer-generated reconstruction of the crash.

▼ The skid marks on a road can show what each vehicle was doing when a crash took place.

Train and Plane Crashes

Whenever a train or plane crashes, the area of the crash is treated in the same way as a crime scene. The whole area is roped off, and only authorized personnel are allowed inside. The job of the forensic team is to establish the cause of the crash. This is normally a complicated job, as the crash could have happened because of faults in the body of the train or plane, negligence by a crew member, or may even be a terrorist attack. For instance, in June 1998, a train crash in Germany killed over 100 people. It was eventually discovered that the crash was caused by metal fatigue in a single wheel.

The Black Box

At the site of a plane crash, one of the first things that happens is the search for the "black box." In fact, every commercial plane has two boxes on board. One of them is a Cockpit Voice Recorder (CVR) which records conversations among the crew (see box). The other is the Flight Data Recorder (FDR) which stores data from the plane's

BUSTED!

One of the planes involved in the 9/11 attacks in 2001 crashed in a field in Pennsylvania. There were no survivors. Forensic teams found the Cockpit Voice Recorder. From the recording, they discovered that the passengers on the plane had attempted to overpower the hijackers. Just prior to the crash, one hijacker told another (who was acting as pilot) to crash the aircraft in order to prevent the passengers from regaining control of it.

instruments. The material in these two boxes is invaluable in determining the cause of a plane crash. Both boxes are usually a bright red or orange color so that they can be found easily.

◀ Crash investigators wearing protective suits examine a train crash in California.

FIRE INVESTIGATIONS

Discovering the cause of a fire, the reasons why it spread, and why people in the fire died is a difficult process. The fire will destroy a lot of the evidence needed in order to find out what actually happened. However, after a fire has been put out, firefighters work with the police and forensic scientists to establish what happened.

The Cause of the Fire

Fires nearly always start in one place, which is known as the point of origin. Fires tend to travel upward and then spread out. This makes it easier for the police to discover where the fire actually started. Fire damage will usually be greater as the investigators get closer to the origin.

Finding the point of origin means that it is easier to discover what caused the fire to start in the first place. Fire investigators will search through all of the burned material at the origin to see if it started the fire. Samples of charred debris are taken back to the lab to see if they will yield any clues. One of the things that they will look for is traces of an

BUSTED!

In February 2009, the Australian state of Victoria suffered one of the worst wildfires in Australian history. There were more than 12 separate major fires and about 400 smaller ones. Over 2,000 houses were destroyed and over 400 people lost their lives. Several people were arrested on suspicion of starting some of the fires deliberately, but only one person, Brendan Sokaluk, has been charged with arson and with causing the death of 11 people.

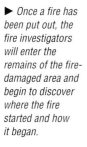

► Once a fire has been put out, the fire investigators will enter the remains of the fire-damaged area and begin to discover where the fire started and how it began.

accelerant. Accelerants are flammable liquids such as gas or paint thinner. The presence of an accelerant would suggest that the fire was started on purpose.

▲ *Some materials burn more easily than others. Until recently, the foam used in soft furniture, such as sofas, was extremely flammable and meant that fires could spread very quickly.*

Fire Testing

Forensic scientists do a large amount of work in the lab to see which materials burn most quickly and which give off the most smoke and toxic gases. A smoke density chamber will measure how much smoke is produced by any burning material. This knowledge is vital because smoke is a killer, and forensic scientists can advise companies that create and furnish buildings about which materials produce the least smoke.

A cone calorimeter is a machine that tests the amount of heat materials give off when they burn, and it also measures the speed at which the heat is created. This is important because the more heat a fire produces, the more intense the fire will be and the faster it spreads.

ON TARGET

Many fire departments have specialists within them that can work with the police and forensic scientists at the site of a fire. Many of these specialists use dogs known as "Fire Investigation Dogs." These dogs are trained to find any suspected accelerants. In the United States, the National Police Canine Association publishes standards for police dog certification.

CASE STUDY: THE LOCKERBIE BOMBING

On Wednesday, December 21, 1988, Pan Am Flight 103 took off from London's Heathrow Airport. Its destination was New York's John F. Kennedy International Airport. Just a few minutes after 7:00 p.m., as the plane was flying over southern Scotland, the plane exploded. All 243 passengers and 16 crew members died instantly. Debris from the plane fell on the small Scottish town of Lockerbie and killed another 11 people, bringing the total number of fatalities to 270. The United Kingdom's Air Accidents Investigation Branch immediately began to investigate the disaster.

Searching for Clues

Over the next few months, over 1,000 police officers and soldiers carried out a fingertip search of the fields and forests around Lockerbie, gathering up the remains of the plane. They were told, "If it isn't growing and it isn't a rock, pick it up." They found over 10,000 items that came from the plane. Evidence of an explosive device was also found, so the investigators knew that the plane had been brought down by a bomb.

◀ This picture shows the fragments of the suitcase that contained the bomb that blew up Pan Am Flight 103. These fragments helped forensic scientists discover what the bomb was made of and how it was set to explode.

ON TARGET

The Air Accidents Investigation Branch was responsible for finding out how and why the plane crashed. However, the suitcase and its contents were investigated by both British and American forensic teams. The American team came from the FBI, and the British team was part of the Defense Evaluation and Research Agency (DERA).

Reconstructing the Plane

All of the parts of the recovered aircraft were taken to Farnborough Airport, the headquarters of the Air Accidents Investigation Branch. There the remains of the plane were put back together again. The investigators found that an area on the left side of the forward cargo hold had been completely ripped apart. This told them that the bomb had been placed there.

Reconstructing the Bomb

Fifty-six pieces of highly charred suitcase were also found. Investigators established that this was the suitcase that held the bomb. Forensic scientists traced tiny amounts of plastic explosives on the fragments of the suitcase to a factory in the Czech Republic. Pieces of a circuit board and a cassette player were also found. This was important because it was known that the same type of cassette player was used by Middle Eastern terrorist groups in bomb making. Clothing fragments from the suitcase were analyzed and traced back to Malta, and

BUSTED!

The Libyan government handed over Abdelbaset Al Megrahi to the British authorities in April 1999. He was tried at a special court in the Netherlands with four Scottish judges. The main evidence against Al Megrahi came from the Maltese shopkeeper who had sold him the clothes found at the crash site. He was found guilty and sentenced to life imprisonment. In August 2009 he was released after it was found that he had cancer.

it was this that first pointed to Libyan involvement. Later investigations in Malta showed that these clothes had been bought by Abdelbaset Al Megrahi. Alleged to be a Libyan intelligence officer, Al Megrahi, who was chief of security for Libyan Arab Airlines, has been the only person to be convicted for the bombing.

◀ The reconstructed remains of Pan Am Flight 103 are still housed in a warehouse by the Air Accidents Investigation Branch.

GLOSSARY

anthropology the scientific study of the biological origins and customs of different groups of people

autopsy a medical examination of a corpse in order to find out the cause of death

black box a fireproof box on commercial planes that record information about each flight; black boxes are used to understand why planes crash.

blood types the division of human blood into four types based on the absence or presence of chemicals in red blood cells

blood spatter patterns the shape of bloodstains at the scene of a crime

carjack to hijack a car or other motor vehicle

clean suit a special item of clothing that covers forensic investigators from head to toe to prevent contamination of the crime scene

comparison microscope a double microscope that allows two samples to be viewed at the same time

contaminate at a crime scene, mixing unwanted substances with evidence

counterfeit imitation or forgery

database a comprehensive collection of data, such as fingerprints or DNA, that is stored on a computer

decomposition when a dead body starts to decay

DNA a long string of molecules found inside the cell; DNA carries information about each individual and is unique to that individual.

DNA fingerprinting also known as DNA profiling; identifying somebody from DNA evidence

entomology the scientific study of insects

expert witness a person who is a specialist in a subject and is asked to present his or her expert opinion at a trial, even though he or she was not at a crime

Federal Bureau of Investigation (FBI) part of the U.S. Department of Justice that conducts investigations into major crimes and helps local police departments with their work

fiber a fine thread or strand

forgery making a copy of something and then claiming it is genuine

geologist somebody who studies rocks and soils

"Golden Hour" the short period of time when a crime scene has not been altered by the weather or human activity

insulin a hormone produced by the pancreas which regulates blood sugar levels; people with diabetes have to inject insulin into their bodies, but an overdose can kill.

larva(e) the stage of an insect's life cycle after it has hatched from an egg; also called maggot

metal fatigue gradual damage to the structure and strength of a piece of metal

molecule a group of chemically combined atoms

pathologist somebody who studies diseases and injuries through an examination of the organs of the body

Polymerase Chain Reaction a method for making copies of a DNA sample so that there is enough DNA to sample

postmortem after death

pupa(e) The stage of an insect's life cycle before it turns into an adult and after the larval stage

Short Tandem Repeat analysis a technique for turning information from a DNA sample into a visual form so that a comparison can be made

striations the unique marks left on a bullet that has been fired

toxicology the scientific study of poisonous chemicals

FURTHER INFORMATION

Books

Ballard, Carol. *Crimebusting!: Identifying Criminals and Victims (Solve That Crime!),* Enslow Publishers, 2010.

Burnscott, Leela. *Fact or Fiction: Looking at Forensic Investigations and Technologies (Forensic Invenstigations),* Smart Apple Media, 2010.

Cooper, Christopher. *Forensic Science (Eyewitness Books),* DK Publishing, 2008.

Innes, Brian. *DNA and Body Evidence (Forensic Evidence),* Sharpe Focus, 2008.

Prokos, Anna. *Guilty by a Hair: Real-life DNA Matches! (24/7: Science Behind the Scenes),* Franklin Watts, 2007.

Spilsbury, Richard. *Bones Speak!: Solving Crimes from the Past (Solve That Crime!),* Enslow Publishers, 2009.

Thompson, Lisa. *Eyes for Evidence: Have You Got What it Takes to be a Forensic Scientist? (On the Job),* Compass Point Books, 2009.

Web Sites

www.fbi.gov/hq/lab/labhome.htm
Information about what the FBI does in the forensic science field.

www2.aafs.org/yfsf
Information for young people who want to work in forensic science.

http://forensics.rice.edu
Background scientific information to the CSI series with plenty of online activities.

www.trutv.com/shows/forensic_files/games/hiddenmine/index.html
Games involving forensic science from the popular TV show Forensic Files.

www.centredessciencesdemontreal.com/static/autopsy/flash.html
Solve a murder using forensic techniques on a web site from the Montreal Science Centre.

http://video.nationalgeographic.com/video/player/science/health-human-body-sci/human-body/body-farm-sci.html
A short video on the National Geographic web site, showing the work of the Body Farm in Tennessee.

www.yourdiscovery.com/crime/_home/index.shtml
Forensic science from the Discovery Channel web site.

Note to parents and teachers: Every effort has been made by the publishers to ensure that these web sites are suitable for children, that they are of the highest educational value, and that they contain no inappropriate or offensive material. However, because of the nature of the Internet, it is impossible to guarantee that the contents of these sites will not be altered. We strongly advise that Internet access is supervised by a responsible adult.

INDEX

SERIES CONTENTS